A Rose, and a Wild Black Horse

To Ursula Nordstrom
who gave me the thought
and Susan Hirshman
who named it
—C.Z.

Written by Charlotte Zolotow
Illustrated by Leslie McGuire

Hooked On Phonics®

First published in 1967 by E. M. Hale and Company by arrangement with Harper & Row, Publishers, Incorporated.
This edition published in 1998 by Gateway Learning Corporation.

ISBN 1-887942-50-5

Guess what I'll do,
said the little boy to his sister.

When I grow up,
I'll break rocks in half for you
with my bare hands.

I'll capture a wild black horse
and tame him for you to ride.

I'll climb a mountain
and bring you a stone from the top.

I'll swim across oceans
and bring you coral from the
bottom of the sea.

I'll do all your math with you.

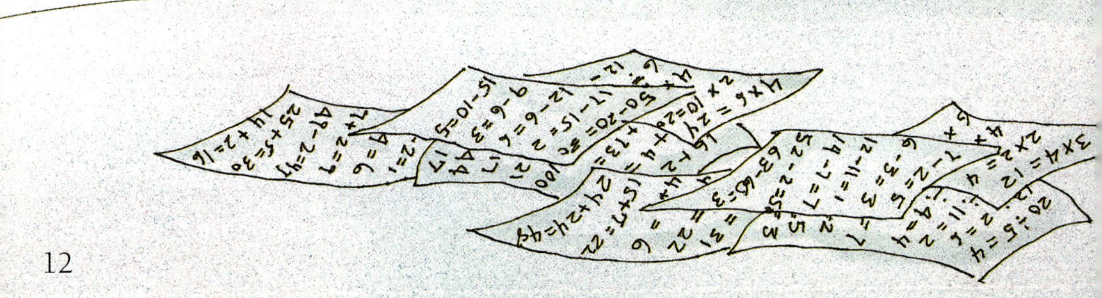

4+4=8
7+7=14
14-8=6
37-5=32
43÷1=43
6x6=36
5x4=20
14-9=5
32-6=26
12÷2=6
42÷7=6
112+63=175
14x12=168
72÷12=6
75x3=225
17-12=5
47-12=35
70-50=20

I'll win the race in the fastest car of all and take you for a windy ride.

I'll build you a bridge that is bigger than any bridge in the world . . .

and a castle to live in.

And I'll pick the pinkest rose in the world for you to smell.

Then I'll bring us a friend
to keep us company…

while we explore the world.